Y0-EDX-878

COLUMBIA ESSAYS ON MODERN WRITERS

NUMBER 7   PRICE $.65

EUGÈNE IONESCO

by Leonard C. Pronko

Infield

The Library of

ST. JOSEPH
COLLEGE

West Hartford, Connecticut

The
Sister Maria Ancilla
Collection

POPE PIUS XII LIB., ST. JOSEPH COLLEGE

3 2528 01331 5470

Eugène Ionesco

by LEONARD C. PRONKO

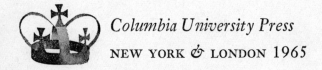

Columbia University Press
NEW YORK & LONDON 1965

COLUMBIA ESSAYS ON MODERN WRITERS is a series of critical studies of English, Continental, and other writers whose works are of contemporary artistic and intellectual significance.

Editor: William York Tindall

Advisory Editors
Jacques Barzun W.T.H. Jackson Joseph A. Mazzeo Justin O'Brien

Eugène Ionesco is Number 7 of the series.

LEONARD C. PRONKO is Associate Professor in the Department of Romance Languages at Pomona College. He is the author of *The World of Jean Anouilh* and *Avant-Garde, the Experimental Theater in France.*

Copyright © 1965 Columbia University Press
Library of Congress Catalog Card Number: 65–16380
Manufactured in the United States of America

Eugène Ionesco

The five years from 1956 to 1961 witnessed the spectacular rise to world renown of an almost unknown playwright who, until 1956, had only been performed in small theaters before limited audiences. In that year a revival of Ionesco's *The Chairs* suddenly attracted attention, receiving high praise from eminent men of letters, including Jean Anouilh. In an article in *Le Figaro* Anouilh claimed that it was a classical work and superior to Strindberg. Less than five years later, Ionesco was being performed in a French national theater before large audiences. He was acclaimed throughout Europe and invited to speak in Finland and America.

Ionesco has had, and continues to have, many detractors, for he is a controversial figure. Of his significance, however, there can be no doubt, for his voice, while strikingly original in its expression, speaks for a large segment of thinking people today, a voice of freedom in a world of conformity. Ionesco's contribution to world dramaturgy has been both in subject and in form.

Born in Slatina, Rumania, in 1912 of a Rumanian father and French mother, Eugène Ionesco spent his formative years in France. It was not until 1925, when he was thirteen, that he returned to Rumania and learned the Rumanian language. After studies at the University of Bucharest he became a teacher of French. At the same time he was writing poetry and criticism. In 1939 he returned to France, where he has lived ever since, with his wife and a daughter born in 1944.

[3]

Ionesco tells us in his journal that he has always written. But it was not until his thirty-sixth year that he began to write for the theater. At that time, having undertaken the study of English conversation by the Assimil method, he was struck by the many elemental truths voiced by the personages introduced in his lesson book—truths we accept as basic to our everyday living and yet rarely reflect upon. Instead of learning English, he began to write a play incorporating the Smiths and Martins whom he had met in his study of English, and thus *The Bald Soprano* (1949) was born.

Ionesco's first play, subtitled an "anti-play," established the simple plot, mechanical dehumanized characters, and exaggeratedly absurd language that were to become the marks of his early plays—characteristics that are still by and large identified with his works. While faithful to his obsessions, Ionesco has not, however, stood still technically, and his later plays show a considerable development, and perhaps a greater understanding of (or concession to) traditional theatrical requirements. In his production to date we can note a gradual transition from the dehumanized to the more human, from the mechanical to the more reflective, from the puzzling to the more readily understood. The early plays depend largely upon mechanical rhythms set up by the characters and their language, in order to suggest the underlying meaninglessness of most of our efforts to act and communicate. The rare moments of lucidity we witness in the Old Man and the Old Woman in *The Chairs* (1951) introduce a more humanly aware character which is to receive greater elaboration in later dramas, reaching full flower in the four Bérengers created in Ionesco's last four plays. Concurrently the language becomes less dizzying in its repetitions, *non sequiturs,* and pure nonsense, approximating more closely the language of everyday life. Some critics have praised the late Ionesco as a dramatist

[4]

who has at last learned how to communicate and to write in acceptable forms, while others would consider his progression a degeneration from the free fantasy of his early work to the more conventional plays like *Rhinoceros* and *The King Dies*.

This itinerary, whether we consider it desirable or not, is traced and commented upon by Ionesco himself in a collection of commentaries and articles, *Notes and Counter Notes*, gathered from many magazines, newspapers, and speeches. They reveal the dramatist as an equally brilliant essayist, adept at explaining his attitudes and defending his practices in language that is lucid and entertaining. They form an extremely valuable accompaniment to the plays, but, as Ionesco, constantly annoyed by his critics and their efforts to explain and interpret, has pointed out time and again, the plays must ultimately stand on their own. And they must stand on their own in two ways. First of all as theatrical experiences, in which each play will itself determine whether it has been successful or not with a particular audience. Second, the plays must stand as dramatic structures, rather than as tracts or sermons in favor of some particular ideology, for Ionesco is diametrically opposed to both Sartre and Brecht, and his only commitment is non-commitment, an open, constantly *disponible*, free attitude which lies at the antipodes of any kind of totalitarianism, whether it be political, religious, artistic, or social.

In his essays Ionesco underlines constantly the freedom of the artist and urges the playwright to explore uninhibitedly the entire terrain of life and dreams, using all the possibilities offered by the stage. The Théâtre Libre of Antoine, he claims, was simply a new slavery, and we must invent, or rather find once again for today, the true Free Theater. Nothing is barred in the theater, he tells us, and in order adequately to reflect life as we know it today we must enrich our artistic expression, infuse it with wonder, with fantasy, with violence too. For we seem to have forgotten that the essence of drama is in exaggeration, magnification. The vocabulary Ionesco employs in his essay "Experience of the Theater" suggests the kind of plays he has in mind: caricature, farce, parody; grotesque, brutal, broad, outrageous, unendurable. "We need to be virtually bludgeoned," he tells us, "into detachment from our daily lives, our habits and mental laziness, which conceal from us the strangeness of the world."

The first bludgeoning offered the French audiences by Ionesco was not really intended to be a play at all, but the author's friends so enjoyed his reading of the dialogue he had concocted that they encouraged him to allow a young troupe to consider it for production. Enthusiasm was so great that the play was immediately put into rehearsal.

Thematically *The Bald Soprano* is *not* a critique of the English bourgeoisie, for Ionesco has affirmed most emphatically that he knew nothing of Englishmen at the time, and only the accident of having been studying English dictated the English setting. His target was, however, the bourgeoisie, but an international, universal type of bourgeois which he has defined as the man of slogans and fixed ideas who is empty and dehumanized because he lives by clichés. The Smiths and Martins, whose evening of chatter we witness, are gross exaggerations of types we know—and even of ourselves, for one of the characteristics of Ionesco's theater is that we may recognize ourselves, or elements of ourselves, in people, situations, and language which are pushed beyond credibility until they explode in a kind of dramatic paroxysm.

But parody of the universal bourgeois is not the only theme of this play, for it makes a trenchant comment on family life, society, the married couple, and language as well. Through the outrageous farce an implicit critique is made of man's discomfort as an animal forced into social situations and attempting to

[6]

communicate by means of a language that has largely broken down.

The Bald Soprano is also a parody of the commercial French theater, the *théâtre de boulevard*, with its conventional situations and shallow psychology. But more than that, it is a daring experiment in theatrical form—perhaps only half-conscious since it was not orginally intended for production—but of extreme importance because it led Ionesco to write a number of plays that have consciously attempted to break the rigid forms of established drama and have exercised a profound influence on young playwrights throughout the world. *The Bald Soprano* has been called abstract or pure theater, for in this play Ionesco has attempted to suppress elements he considered extraneous to the dramatic experience, such as plot, psychology, specific ideas. Instead we have what he describes as "a construction made up of a series of states of consciousness, or situations, which grow more intense, more concentrated, and then knit together either to be unraveled or to end in inextricable and unendurable confusion." Epics, movies, and novels tell stories, Ionesco states, but the theater should be a revelation of another sort. *The Bald Soprano,* and indeed most of Ionesco's one-act plays, are built about a simple situation which, beginning in more or less realistic terms, slowly is disarticulated, exploded, exaggerated until something monstrous and violent is achieved. This situation, or a state of euphoria or anguish, is pushed to the extreme, intensified beyond the point of return. Consequently there are rarely denouements of a conventional kind. From the quiet evening at the Smiths' home, we move through a slow accelerando to the recognition scene of the Martins, build to the arrival of the fireman, increasing both speed and intensity as the tales told by the characters become less and less comprehensible, ending finally with the chaotic cries of the characters uttering nonsense syllables,

[7]

frustrated completely in their efforts to communicate, and reduced to a subhuman level.

Ionesco is attempting in his early plays to focus our attention on the theatrical structure itself, rather than on any
specific ideological content. Just as an abstract painting deals
with form and color rather than with recognizable objects,
these dramas deal with the forms and colors of dramatic art,
reducing the recognizable human content to a minimum. Instead of ordinary people revealing a more or less real psychology, we see grotesque robots, people reduced to a mechanical
exterior, language no longer purporting to communicate a
specific meaning, and situations that seem to have no motiva-
tion and to lead to no conclusion. Like blobs of paint on a
canvas, the characters are simply there.

There is, of course, an important difference. Whereas the
painting is constructed from colors and forms that have no
explicit meaning, plays are constructed, at least partly, with
words that do have explicit meanings, and no matter how non-
sensically they are used they are bound to communicate something of the meaning we usually associate with the word.
Moreover, the human presence cannot be divorced from the
stage, and so the play can never reach the level of abstraction
of a painting or of music. Ionesco, and many of the experimental playwrights today—most notably Jean Tardieu—are
trying to work in new ways with the structures of drama and
see just how they can follow the developments of other arts.

A corollary of this direction taken by drama is the greater
role played by nonverbal elements in the production such as
properties, scenery, and costumes. Such techniques Ionesco
was to develop in his later plays, but already in *The Bald
Soprano* we can see that language is being used as a kind of
property rather than in the usual literary way. The words and
sentences become brittle and take on an almost solidified exist-

ence of their own. From the very start, in the stage directions, Ionesco repeats the adjective "English" until it becomes both meaningless and comical: "A middle-class English interior, with English armchair. An English evening. Mr. Smith, an Englishman, seated in his English armchair and wearing English slippers, is smoking his English pipe and reading an English newspaper, near an English fire." Like any word too often repeated, it begins to impress us as a pattern of sounds; that is, by its physical presence. The same phenomenon occurs repeatedly: in Mrs. Smith's preoccupation with "the oil from the grocer across the street" as compared with "the oil from the grocer at the bottom of the street"; in the discussion devoted to Bobby Watson; the mechanical reactions of the Martins in their scene of discovery; the arguments regarding the Fireman at the door. The final scene shows language as object triumphant. At first it is comprehensible, however bizarre:

MRS. MARTIN. I can buy a pocketknife for my brother, but you can't buy Ireland for your grandfather.
MR. SMITH. One walks on his feet, but one heats with electricity or coal.
MR. MARTIN. He who sells an ox today, will have an egg tomorrow.

It soon forsakes all semblance of sense:

MR. SMITH. The pope elopes! The pope's got no horoscope. The horoscope's bespoke.
MRS. MARTIN. Bazaar, Balzac, bazooka!
MR. MARTIN. Bizarre, beaux-arts, brassieres!

This materialization of the nonphysical leads to the proliferation of matter, which in Ionesco's subsequent work is to play such an important role.

Although Ionesco eschews a particular ideology in his plays, he does hope to make some kind of statement regarding man

[9]

and his situation. If he is strenuously opposed to the political commitment of Brecht and Sartre, he is just as critical of the superficial commercial plays that treat theater as pure entertainment. For, if drama is to have a lasting value, it must take some position on fundamental issues. But since it is drama, and not philosophy or sociology, it must take its position in a general, indirect way, rather than attempting to direct the thoughts and attitudes of its audience. Ionesco is fond of pointing out that the other arts have not been confused with ideologies—no one dreams of putting philosophy into music, and we like to think that we have gone beyond the stage where we require political or psychological comment in a painting—and yet we seem to feel that the theater must teach us something.

Art, Ionesco has said in one of his aphoristic statements, is the realm of passion, not of pedagogy. And the source of his own dramas lies deep in the unconscious of the dramatist. When he begins to write, he has no fixed purpose, and is unaware of the direction he will follow. It is only after he has created a play that he begins to understand it himself, he claims. Welling from the subconscious, but controlled by an artistic instinct, the plays embody the fundamental obsessions of Ionesco the man. And because they are his own fundamental obsessions he feels that they possess a certain universality, for all of us are preoccupied basically with the same problems: the meaning of life, the meaning of death, and how to face each. In addition to these general themes, there are of course a number of secondary themes that form part of the main one: the inability to communicate on any really profound level (we can all understand "Pass the salt, please," but when I say, "I love her," or "I'm dying," who indeed can understand me at all?), the difficulty of living together as family or as man and wife, the constant encroachment of the other.

[10]

In an early essay Ionesco points out that there are two fundamental feelings at the origin of all his work: one of lightness, evanescence, strangeness, and the other of heavy, gray opacity. When the former dominates, he writes comedy, and when the latter is foremost, drama. Most often, however, they both occur within the same play, which frequently starts in an atmosphere of light and happiness and ends in silence, opacity, and death—what Ionesco has described as the victory of the antispiritual forces. This leads, of course, to an interweaving of the tragic and comic, for as Ionesco envisions it, the two are inextricable. In fact, he is not certain what differentiates them, for the comic is the intuition of the absurdity of a universe in which man has neither dignity nor absolutes, and therefore a more starkly depressing universe than that of tragedy, which confers upon man a certain nobility and meaning in the midst of his defeat.

Ionesco's theater, like that of the other experimental dramatists writing in France today, the so-called theater of the absurd, constantly mixes the tragic and the comic, and in such a way that there is no clear distinction, for we are meant to shudder at some of the comedy, and to laugh at the tragedy of man's situation, which is treated in derisory terms. This laughter at our own tragic situation gives us a certain objectivity, and is perhaps the only reaction possible in a world that has destroyed our faith in absolutes.

Ionesco then is writing metaphysical drama. It is not, however, a drama that expounds a metaphysical system, for all systems are abhorrent to this advocate of freedom and individual thinking. We are afraid of freedom of thought, he says, just as we are afraid of a play that is too tragic or despairing. A large group of Ionesco's critics find him negative, and constantly urge him to give us a "positive" message; as though the positive message were not the most negative of gifts, for it denies our own freedom to decide for ourselves.

In a brilliant preface to Ionesco's first volume of plays, published in 1954, the young critic Jacques Lemarchand noted that there are some people who are constantly harassed by their intellect—it is like a little spartan fox incessantly gnawing at their entrails and asking, "What is it about?" From the start, he says, such people were annoyed by Ionesco. They were asked to see a play called *The Bald Soprano,* and were unable to find a soprano of any kind in it. Thus warned, they came to see *The Lesson* quite prepared, but were bewildered again, for this time what they saw was indeed a lesson. Among them were certainly two of France's most influential—and most conservative—drama critics, Robert Kemp and Jean-Jacques Gautier. Outraged, abused, they branded Ionesco "an insignificant curiosity of today's theater, a hoaxer, a mystifier." In the United States Maurice Valency has condemned the "new theater," of which Ionesco is a part, for its formlessness, its forgetfulness of Aristotelean concepts. He feels that it leads to moral stagnation, for it shows "man's insignificance and his grotesque plight between an imaginary hell and an imaginary heaven."

With artists who are so close to us it is no doubt rash to make any such categorical pronouncements. What Ionesco's detractors describe as negative, dehumanized, immature, his admirers have called "implacably human." Ionesco sees man as the "creating animal," and therefore he leaves each of us our humanity, our creative freedom. "It seems to me absurd," he writes,

to ask a dramatist to produce a bible, a way to salvation; it is absurd to think for a whole world and give it some automatic philosophy: a playwright poses problems. . . . Even a stupid man is worth more than an intelligent, educated ass: an unworkable solution one has found for oneself is infinitely more valuable than a ready-made ideology that stops men from thinking.

It is difficult to see how such an outlook can lead to moral stagnation, since it points the way to a vital, meaningful morality based on self-discovery and lucidity. Such a faith in the human potential reveals Ionesco as profoundly optimistic.

There is perhaps nothing new in these attitudes, or in the desire to create a theater of metaphysical awareness. What is new, however, is that Ionesco, Beckett, and a few others writing in France at mid-century, have attempted to give to their plays the very shape of their ideas. This is why Ionesco says that he is preoccupied with the theatrical structure itself. If our world is one in which people strike us as inhuman, then let us place robots on the stage. If we feel that the physical aspects of life deny us the full development of our spiritual potential, then by all means let that be reflected in a play whose décor or properties slowly dominate the characters. If language is worn out, then let us show the solidified forms of that language as cliché and slogan, or words reduced to pure agglomerates of sound. The result is metaphysics transformed for the theater, and a theater transformed by metaphysics but remaining theater: a source of experience and not of indoctrination.

The Lesson (1950) shows us the dangers of indoctrination: a Professor gives a lesson in mathematics and philology to a young Student eager to earn her "total doctorate." At first apologetic and meek, as he begins to impose his ideas upon the Student the Professor becomes a monster, until at last he kills the young girl with a metaphorical knife. She is his fortieth victim this day. There are sexual connotations throughout the play, and the action suggests the immorality of any attempt to impose one's own ideology or wishes upon another, whether it be in the field of pedagogy, politics, or personal life. From a more or less meaningful relationship of teacher and student at

[13]

the start, the two end up as animal and object, executioner and victim.

The satire of language is more explicit in *The Lesson* than in Ionesco's first play, for the Professor's lecture in philology purports to show how languages that sound alike, and are indeed indistinguishable, are in fact profoundly different. For example, when a Frenchman says "my capital" he means something completely different from what a Spaniard would mean by the same words. The Professor himself is an illustration of how words crack and disintegrate under the strain of use, no longer tools for communication but instruments of torture and imprisonment:

I'm speaking of the neo-Spanish languages which one is able to distinguish from each other, however, only thanks to their distinctive characteristics, absolutely indisputable proofs of their extraordinary resemblances, which renders indisputable their common origins, and which, at the same time, differentiates them profoundly—through the continuation of the distinctive traits which I've just cited.

His lecture, sounding curiously learned, is in actuality a garbled mess of nonsense, but based upon the formulas we associate with learning, and which are its very opposite.

Jack, or The Submission (1950) shows Jack, recalcitrant individualist, finally admitting that he likes fried potatoes with bacon—tantamount to an admission that he accepts the rules of society—accepting a fiancée with three noses, Roberta, after having rejected her two-nosed sister, also named Roberta (both of them "only daughters" of the same parents). In its sequel *The Future is in Eggs* (1951) Jack and Roberta, after a lengthy romantic interlude, finally give in to their families' exhortation to raise children, and while Roberta lays eggs offstage, Jack incubates them before our very eyes.

These two plays, very close in spirit to *The Bald Soprano*, remind us of Ionesco's admiration for Alfred Jarry and the surrealists; for the gross social satire, neologisms and puns, rejection of any pretense at realism, and stress on the animal in man all recall the great precursor of theater of the absurd and the seminal movement of the 1920s which, while it gave rise to no great drama itself, was so important in preparing the way for today's avant-garde writers.

Like the Bobby Watsons who proliferate in the dialogue of *The Bald Soprano* and suggest the anonymity of people who have the same name and are entirely indistinguishable, Jack's relatives all bear his name or one of its diminutives, while Roberta's family all bear variants of her name. Words, too, are reduced to anonymity as Roberta tells Jack that in her *chat*eau all things are called *chat* (cat), whether they be chairs, people, or lemonade. Like the quarreling couples at the end of Ionesco's first play, like the Professor at the end of *The Lesson*, the characters here once again end up even more dehumanized than at the start. As the curtain falls on *Jack* we hear the beastly groans of the relatives, and see the pale three-nosed face of the fiancée and her *nine*-fingered hand undulating in reptilian fashion.

The Future is in Eggs concludes with the clucking sounds of Roberta as she lays eggs offstage, accompanied by the families' cries of "Long live the white race!" In the latter play the stage is cluttered with eggs which, while they may be the promise of opportunists, nationalists, populists, chemists, existentialists, drunks, pencils, pens, matches, and above all omelettes to come, are in their egg state peculiarly inhuman, a mass of matter threatening to cover poor Jack. Here is the first instance of the proliferation of matter that is to play so important a role in succeeding plays. We have already seen language used as an object, but here physical matter itself, encroaching on the human presence, threatens to take over, and reveals by

[15]

its very presence the victory of the antispiritual forces that the characters have all too clearly embraced.

The Master, Maid to Marry, and *The Motor Show*, forming part of a series of seven sketches (the others are lost or, at any rate, unpublished), are brief spoofs of love, the family, demagoguery, etc., couched in the usual platitudes, and mechanical behavior. Each ends with a surprise, as the awaited Master arrives without a head, the "maid" to marry turns out to be a man, and the new automobile that is carried off is actually a young lady.

It is difficult to believe that these almost flippant little sketches date from the same year as *The Chairs*, which shows an immense advance over Ionesco's earlier work both in the creation of character and in breadth of meaning. No doubt the incredible automatons of his earliest plays are amusing, and are even made to carry their burden of meaning, but if Ionesco was to appeal to a larger audience, to write works of greater profundity and of broader implication, it was necessary to pass beyond the stage of purely mechanical beings and impart a certain degree of humanity to his personages, so that the spectator might feel moved to some kind of personal identification with them. In *The Chairs* he has done just this, but he has not created conventional stage characters, for they still bear to a large degree that mechanized imprint. There are sufficient feeling, individuality, and pathos, however—brought about chiefly by moments of self-awareness—to arouse an emotional response from the public. With the exception of a few characters in *Victims of Duty* and *Amédée*, we must wait six years until the Bérenger plays to find creations of comparable dimensions.

Structurally the play is extremely simple and resembles the earlier ones in its progression from apparent meaning to nonsense. But whereas the earlier plays had ended with the dehumanized characters even more inhuman and reduced to animal sounds and movements, *The Chairs* leads beyond that to absolute silence and absence. The absence-presence dichotomy which forms its major theme stands again for that victory of matter—a phenomenon that only too clearly manifests its absence of living meaning—over what should be a vital, human presence. The central metaphor of the play, that of the chairs themselves—society and others who separate us from each other and from "the Emperor"—is brilliantly original in conception and in treatment. Convinced like most of his contemporaries in the avant-garde that a play is much more than a text, Ionesco attempts to use the visual as well as the aural aspects of theater. The dilapidated décor, the seven doors leading everywhere and nowhere used indiscriminately by the actors, the ghostly green light, and above all the sight of the chairs, painfully brought in by the old couple, and finally crowding the Old Man and Woman to opposite sides of the stage—these are exciting adjuncts to the text and help to put across the author's perception in strictly theatrical ways.

An Old Man and Woman have lived a lonely mediocre life on an island. Encouraged by his wife, who coddles him, and convinced he has something significant to say, the Old Man has invited all remaining human beings to hear his "message" before he dies. As the guests arrive we note that they are invisible, but a chair is brought for each, and finally, when the stage is completely cluttered, after having greeted and chatted with their guests, the old couple leap to their death in the sea, leaving the Orator (the only other visible character) to deliver the priceless message. He is a mute and can only grunt—for what really profound message is communicable, and who can discover the secret of life for us? He exits, and for a long moment we watch the empty stage, and hear the waves washing about the walls of the house.

This final scene, when well presented, constitutes an extremely impressive theatrical moment, for it exposes the spectator to a theatricalized experience of nothingness. "The play was written *for* this ending," Ionesco declares. In performance, the blackboard business mentioned in the text is usually omitted and the Orator simply bows and makes his exit after his futile attempts to deliver the "message." "The very last scene must be very long," Ionesco says, "the sound of murmuring, of wind, and water, should be heard for a very long time, as though coming from nothing, coming from the void."

Lest the reader or viewer should assume that the "invisible" guests are simply figments of a senile imagination, Ionesco stresses the importance of the murmuring heard from the invisible crowd after the old people have disappeared. What he is striving for is "an effect beyond reason, upsetting logic, and raising fresh doubts." No one in the play is any less real than anyone else, he tells us, but obviously a drama cannot be created with totally absent characters (although it has been tried) and therefore the Old Man and Woman are visible and audible. The physical presence of the Orator also seemed the only way to overcome an otherwise insoluble technical problem.

In addition to the social commentary implicit in the earlier plays, *The Chairs* possesses a more evident metaphysical import of some depth. There is no effort to develop a particular viewpoint, but beyond the parody of society, conversation, and the couple, there is a suggestion of man's ultimate meaninglessness and the uselessness of his existence, since at last he must die having said nothing, having found nothing. Ionesco's "contrapuntal treatment of lies, illusions, ancient guilts and broken dreams," Professor Lamont points out, "illustrates effectively the insubstantial bases on which we build our lives." Whether we agree with the philosophy such an outlook implies, we cannot deny the dramatic effectiveness of Ionesco's vision as it is realized in *The Chairs*, surely one of his most successful plays.

The Chairs announces what might be called a second period in Ionesco's development. The major plays between it and *The Killer* will depend less upon the author's command of linguistic play, and more upon the visible proliferation of objects, which now becomes his principal means of communicating his idea.

Victims of Duty (1952) is interesting as a statement of purpose, for here Ionesco speaks more explicitly than he has in any play before it. Dramatically it is perhaps less interesting, and yet the experiment with the unconscious is worthy of note. Choubert and his wife Madeleine (and through them the couple is once again satirized) are interrupted in their arguments by the arrival of a Detective in search of a certain Mallot. Choubert sets out to find him, exploring his subconscious, which is represented onstage by swimming and crawling on the floor, climbing chairs, etc. As in the prelogical state, people have no fixed identity, and Choubert's relationship to his wife and the Detective shifts curiously. At times they even watch his search as though it were a performance, commenting on the sad state of the theater today. After an unsuccessful search, Choubert is forced to chew and swallow mouthfuls of bread while his wife serves coffee to the Detective in innumerable cups which cover the sideboard. Choubert's friend, Nicolas D'Eu, kills the Detective, after defending a new kind of irrational theater against the Aristotelean one represented by the Detective:

The theatre of my dreams would be irrationalist. . . . You see, my dear fellow, the contemporary theatre doesn't reflect the cultural tone of our period, it's not in harmony with the general

[19]

drift of the other manifestations of the modern spirit. . . . We'll get rid of the principle of identity and unity of character and let movement and dynamic psychology take its place.

The play we have just witnessed is, of course, built along the lines described by Nicolas. Earlier in the play, Choubert, talking with his wife, declared that there had been little evolution in the theater. Whether it be Greek tragedy, medieval morality, or modern naturalist drama, a play is essentially a riddle, a kind of "investigation brought to a successful conclusion. There's a riddle, and it's solved in the final scene. Sometimes earlier. You seek, and then you find. Might as well give the game away at the start." In *Victims of Duty* the game is never given away. Using the form of a detective play, Ionesco refuses us an answer. The Detective is once again the familiar figure of the totalitarian, dehumanized to a degree where, a "victim of duty," he can only obey authority. He dies, uttering the frightening cry "Long live the white race!" The nightmarish intensity of certain scenes reminds us that Ionesco's drama is a theatrical realization of his own dreams and fears. In this particular play, however, the distance from dream to drama is perhaps not sufficient.

If *Victims of Duty* is too specific to be theatrically effective from beginning to end, *The New Tenant* (1953) is quite the opposite, for it is just short of pantomime. The dialogue between the Concierge and the newly arrived tenant is reduced to a minimum. Like most of Ionesco's concierges, this one carries on a monologue with herself, grunting, complaining, questioning, answering, revealing her frighteningly inhuman mind and her readiness to think in clichés. Proliferating matter triumphs as the New Occupant's furniture is carried in by the moving men. Carefully he indicates where each piece is to be placed. Slowly, as in *The Chairs,* the stage is covered with furniture, at last hiding the little man behind chests of drawers, screens, chairs. The entire city, we are told, is filled with furniture, the subway and the river are crammed to overflowing, marking of course the victory of the antispiritual. And yet we laugh, for the parody is extreme and the situation exaggerated to unlikely proportions. But our laughter is reflective, for when we think of the furniture (or the chairs or teacups) as standing for something else, we realize the profound truth of Ionesco's extravagant farce. Victims of duty, of roles imposed by society, or of our own habits of thought, how many of us bury ourselves ceremoniously, surrounded by the familiar objects of our everyday life? Like the New Occupant we might well simply ask the movers to turn off the light, and relax into our living death.

Amédée, or How to Get Rid of It (1953?), Ionesco's first full-length play, deals with a familiar situation: the problems of the couple. Amédée and his wife Madeleine, after many years of marriage, are apparently quite unhappy together. Their incompatability is represented in one of Ionesco's most ingenious, significant, and dramatically effective images, that of a huge cadaver which husband and wife discovered in their bedroom some years ago. It is afflicted with the dreadful disease of the dead, "geometric progression," and is growing at such a rate that by the end of the first act it has knocked down the door of the living room, and by the end of Act Two it has grown across the room, shoving Amédée and Madeleine into a corner. Their dead, now meaningless, relationship is slowly destroying them, strangling them.

Frightened lest someone discover this body, they have closed themselves up in the apartment, refusing even to accept mail, and fetching their groceries by a basket lowered from the window. Amédée has been writing a play for many years, but has not gotten beyond the first two lines. His wife, embittered by his lack of ambition, works at a telephone switch-board set up at one end of the apartment. The couple are tragically aware of their wasted lives, and this relative lucidity leads us to pity them. Like the old couple in *The Chairs* they elicit an emotional response from the audience.

The situations he creates allow Ionesco to treat a number of favorite themes, but all of them in the usual indirect fashion rather than approaching them explicitly, as he had in *Victims of Duty*: the difficulty of writing, incommunicability, incomprehension, incompatability, cliché. Because of the more human characterization of Amédée and Madeleine there is less opportunity for the mechanized behavior and dead language, but they still play some role, as indeed they continue to do through Ionesco's penultimate drama. With extreme economy of means, in two acts he manages to say a great deal. In the last act, however, the play seems to fall apart, for the unity of the first part is destroyed when Amédée, finally forced to get rid of the cumbersome body, pulls it out the window and down to the Seine. On the way he meets soldiers, prostitutes, police-men, and townspeople, and the small closed world of the couple suddenly opens. The play ends, for once, with that feeling of euphoria that is so often vanquished in Ionesco's universe, and Amédée, freed from his wife, clinging to the image of his dead love, flies up into the night sky.

Amédée was written first as a short story, "Oriflamme," and then adapted for the theater. The same is true of all Ionesco's full-length plays, with the exception of the last, *The King Dies. The Killer* is derived from "The Colonel's Photograph," *Rhinoceros* and *The Pedestrian of the Air* from tales bearing the same names as the dramatic versions. What is interesting when comparing the theater texts with the original short stories, to which they are remarkably similar, is the fact that all the stories are written in the first person. This helps us to realize to what a degree Ionesco's plays are indeed "first-person" plays, and the characters and situations he has created, ones with which he identifies himself personally—particularly, of course, the main character through whose mouth the tale is told. Amédée and the various Bérenger characters are, in some ways at least, Ionesco himself. The last of these stories, "Slime," although it would not appear to lend itself to dramatization for the stage, may well end up as a film scenario. As a matter of fact, the death of King Bérenger in *The King Dies* is a realization of this tale in different terms.

The Picture (1954), with its theme of the destruction of spiritual values, looks back to earlier productions, and by its treatment of metamorphosis looks forward to *Rhinoceros*. The first part shows a poor young painter attempting to sell his work to a crude, materialistic Gros Monsieur (a kind of incarnation of Ubu as a businessman) who refuses to look at the painting until the price is settled, and at last succeeds in having the painter pay *him* for keeping the painting. The second part shows the Businessman hanging his painting, and finally transforming his ugly, lame sister into a beautiful princess, like the one in the painting, simply by shooting at her. He does the same for a neighbor; and the young painter, when he returns, is transformed into a Prince Charming. Only the Businessman remains ugly and unrefined by any transformation. Whether we see any serious meaning in this "guignol," it is interesting for the uses it attempts to make of the theater, incorporating the gross farce and slapstick of early films, the tricks of circus and music hall, surrealist fun, and the usual Ionesco parody and platitude into a kind of gratuitous pattern, existing as much for effects as it does for meaning.

Improvisation, or The Shepherd's Chameleon (1955), on the contrary, is not gratuitous at all, and is the most explicit state-

[23]

ment of his theatrical concept in dramatic form that Ionesco has yet given. The French title, *l'Impromptu de l'Alma*, relates it to works of Molière and Giraudoux in which they attempted to expose their dramatic credos in more direct fashion than the conventional play permits. Ionesco is trying to write a play when he is interrupted first by one Bartholomeus, then by another, and finally by a third, all three of them "doctors in theatrology." In his three doctors Ionesco derides several of his critics, the various "isms" and "ologies" which have at one time or another attempted to bend him their way, and of course his favorite targets, the boulevard theater and Brecht. The Bartholomeuses would like their author to be conventional, to write popular (that is to say, proletarian leftist) theater, to teach a lesson, to use the alienation technique of Brecht. Obviously the play is not important, but only what the critics make of it. As they try to drum their ideas into him, Ionesco begins braying like a donkey, until his Maid, the voice of reason, breaks down the door and drives away the doctors. At this point Ionesco dons spectacles and begins to address the audience, criticizing his critics, their narrowness and insistence upon limiting the liberty of the creator who, he feels, can be the only true witness to his age, and only honestly so when he is left completely free. His own theater, he tells us, is the scenic projection of his own inner obsessions. As he begins to assume a rather doctoral tone himself, his Maid slips a doctor's robe upon him, and the curtain falls. At this stage, Ionesco is still able to see himself objectively and to laugh at his own efforts to dogmatize. In an interview given in 1960 he admits that this happens less often now and that he tends to take his own pronouncements more seriously, realizing at the same time that it is a trap.

Improvisation appears to mark a rupture with the earlier style of Ionesco. Not a clean break, certainly, for many stylistic devices from the earlier plays are still employed. But the four plays that follow are all long plays which show a considerable development in the story line, contain at least one character with a more realistic psychology than we have seen until now, and present ideas in a somewhat more explicit way. Since 1957 Ionesco seems to be attempting a renewal of some sort, but the direction he is taking strikes one as less experimental than the paths he had trod heretofore. Despite his declaration that he has been influenced by neither public nor critics, we cannot help wondering whether he has not made an attempt to reach a larger public by writing less "difficult" plays. Indeed, in the preface to *Notes and Counter Notes* he admits that he cannot help thinking of his critics as he writes. This is bound to be reflected in his manner of writing.

The Killer (1957) follows a route diametrically opposed to that of *Amédée*, as indeed most of the long plays do. While *Amédée* begins with a feeling of oppression, heaviness, and opacity, and ends with the euphoria that is described metaphorically by Amédée's escape into the night sky, *The Killer* begins with an evocation of the radiant city in which all men seem destined to be happy, and ends in darkness, silence, death. The décor of the first act is suggested by lights, brightness, clarity; it seems a gay spring day. The last act shows us twilight, dusk, the nightfall of man's life. There is a strong mythical feeling in this play and the characters themselves have an archetypal strength, even in their weakness, and the metaphysical adventure of man in search of his lost paradise is suggested through the efforts of Bérenger to make life bearable by destroying death.

Despite the length of the play, it is still what Ionesco would call traditional and classical: "a simple idea, an equally simple development and a neat ending." In the first act Bérenger visits the radiant city and is overcome with joy at having discovered

[25]

so perfect, so happy a place, until he is told that the Killer murders people here every day. In the second act Bérenger returns home, finds his sick friend Edward waiting for him, and recognizes in the latter's briefcase the contents of the Killer's famous briefcase, including his identity card, note-books, and maps. With these he sets out for the police station. Act Three shows his efforts to reach the police, frustrated first by Edward's loss, or forgetfulness, of his briefcase, which con-tains the proof, then by a political rally and a traffic jam, and finally by his lonely encounter with the Killer before whom he ultimately recognizes his defeat.

The radiant city of Act One, it soon becomes clear to us, is simply too perfect. It possesses the calm and perfection of death itself, for the windows of the houses are all closed, the streets are empty, and every aspect of life is so overorganized and regulated, so mechanized, that no spontaneity can remain. The Architect, who is also Commissioner of the little city within a city, has *all* the dossiers in his keeping, he carries about a small telephone to keep in touch with other depart-ments. Indeed his bureaucracy is such that no total human response is any longer possible. The happy city is in reality the terminus, the depot of the street car that is life, for all the lines lead here we are told. And, conveniently, right outside the walls of the city there is a cemetery.

Life is struggle and suffering, to close our eyes to this is to become as dehumanized as is the Architect who can calmly munch his sandwich while he hears of the murder of his secre-tary, all the while claiming that one must see the good side of things, for after all these murders do allow journalists to earn their living.

The gray city of living people—or apparently living—con-trasts heavily with the light décor of the radiant city. The worn old furniture of Bérenger's room seems to crowd out

[26]

human life, just as did the furniture of the New Occupant, and the empty stage of the first half of the act suggests again that absence-presence dichotomy that is so important a part of *The Chairs*. For twenty minutes or more the only human presence on stage is that of Edward, sick, tubercular, hiding his shriveled arm as he crouches in a chair in the dark, invisible to all. The only movement and sounds come from the outside, as we watch and hear life going on in the street. But it is a derisory life, a mechanized, nonsensical kind of existence reflected in the voices of the concierge, a drunk, several old men, a teacher, and assorted passers-by. Narrow, prejudiced, unthinking attitudes are reflected in the comments of the concierge; suffering, death, disease, senility, in the voices of the old men. Life must be organized, other voices tell us, even our moments of rest must be planned. Yapping dogs, passing machines, the crisscrossing of conversation all combine to create an effect, which while amusing, has depressing connotations.

Bérenger, disappointed in his belief that he had discovered a happiness possible in life, is determined to find the Killer and save mankind. Like his avatar in *Rhinoceros*, he refuses to capitulate. He hopes and dreams, and is distinguished by his refusal to accept what we have come to call the human condition. In his own little way, he is a rebel and a nonconformist, and reminds us of the basic humanistic attitudes of Ionesco himself. Indeed, it seems not incorrect to identify with the dramatist himself, in a general way, the four Bérenger characters who are the heroes of these last plays. They possess a depth, a reality, a humanity, a pathetic truth which none of his earlier characters shared, and Ionesco himself has told us how persistently Bérenger intrudes himself in the author's thoughts, and will not allow himself to be used or dismissed.

If death and suffering are part of the order of the world, then there comes a time when men can no longer accept things

[27]

as they are, and Bérenger places himself on their side against the absurd forces of the universe, reminding us of Camus's hero of the absurd, and of the fact that Ionesco was an ardent admirer of Camus, and no doubt possesses a close spiritual kinship with him. Although Ionesco has constantly opposed the idea of commitment, it is a political commitment he refuses, for in a broader sense he is obviously committed to man's freedom. The wise man just keeps quiet, Edward says, but Bérenger-Ionesco chooses folly.

Bérenger's friend Edward is a strange and perplexing character, for he seems actually unwilling to help Bérenger denounce the Killer. His briefcase, crammed so full of objects identified with the assassin would seem to implicate him in the crime. Indeed this is precisely what Ionesco wishes to suggest, for Edward's indifference makes him as guilty as all of us who refuse to do our utmost to alleviate human suffering. The Architect carries a briefcase like Edward's, and so do most of the characters we meet in the last act, as though it were a brand, marking our culpability. Only the naïve and innocent Bérenger goes empty-handed.

The proliferation of briefcases continues, of course, the device made famous by earlier plays, and reminds us again of the victory of the antispiritual. It is an attenuated use of the device however, for by now Ionesco's leading character, having become more human, his dialogue more explicit, the dramatist depends less upon nonverbal elements to put across his meaning. The dialogue itself, at times recalling earlier plays by the use of nonsensical associations, now differs little from that used in more conventional kinds of drama. Several themes are presented rather directly in Bérenger's dialogue.

Mother Pipe, the political demagogue of Act Three, is one of the first manifestations of direct political satire in Ionesco's theater, and is an indication of the direction he has taken since

1955. Her language is made up of absurd slogans and catch phrases taken from the Communists, the Brechtians, political theater addicts, etc. At times the satire becomes too obvious, as when the drunkard, until this moment quite delightfully tipsy, gives a too logical exposition of his ideas: that the true revolutionaries are not politicians but scientists and artists. Previously one of the hallmarks of Ionesco and his confreres in the avant-garde had been their use of suggestion, indirection. It was not possible to choose a particular speech or set of speeches and say that they set forth the ideas of the author. Rather, it was necessary to find the meaning of the play and the attitudes of the author in the entire texture of the play. It is therefore disconcerting to find in the Bérenger plays an occasional sentence or paragraph that one feels is an explicit expression of Ionesco's outlook, almost a quote from one of his lucid essays.

The entire last act reads rather like one of Kafka's fables of frustration, and reminds us that Ionesco was stimulated by both Kafka and the Marx brothers. The old man looking for the Danube in Paris; the inhuman gigantic policemen, prisoners of their social function, threatening and sadistic, refusing to do anything but direct traffic; the pathetically gentle soldier with his bunch of flowers—all recall a world of dream or nightmare. And most of all, the frightening apparition of the Killer as Bérenger wends his solitary way through the dark countryside to the police station.

The final scene, a lengthy monologue by Bérenger, which Ionesco tells us is a little play in itself, shows the complete demolition of Bérenger's intentions, vanquished by the cold, silent, cynical obstinacy of the Killer. Reasoning with such good faith, seeing both sides of each question (as indeed Ionesco insists he himself does), Bérenger succeeds only in convincing himself that ultimately either one of them may be right. If there is no reason to kill, there is *ultimately* no reason not to kill either. At first energetic in his search for the police station, where he intends to denounce the Killer, Bérenger is soon assailed by doubts and fears. He tries to excuse himself, and finally decides to return home and wait till the next day, since it is already so late. It is at this moment that he turns and sees the Killer (Ionesco also suggests the possibility of staging the scene with no visible Killer). Bérenger feels huge, confident, vigorous before the tiny one-eyed Killer. In his greatness of spirit he says he wishes to try to understand the Killer's attitude—apparently a fatal mistake when one's opponent is inhuman. From a desire to understand, he passes to a confession of brotherly feeling and love, and trots out all sorts of platitudes to persuade the Killer, offering to buy him new shoes and help find him work. Not realizing that this is a killer without wages (and such is the French title of the play), Bérenger points out that "crime doesn't pay."

In the face of the Killer's silence, Bérenger is forced to make answers for him, and slowly he almost comes to see his opponent's viewpoint. He admits that he too sometimes doubts the use of life. Clearly he is weakening. Finally he kneels before the assassin and begs him to change his ways, admitting that "we" may have been unjust to him. All sense of judgment gone, he can only plead until in a burst of anger he aims his guns at the Killer, who stands there with knife drawn. But his guns are useless, and as the curtain falls Bérenger asks desperately, "What can we do?"

The Killer is not necessarily Death. He is an image who suggests the killer Death, just as the briefcase in Edward's possession does not mean that Edward *is* the Killer, but associates Edward with him metaphorically. Although the meaning of *The Killer* strikes us as more explicit than that of, say, *The Chairs* or *The New Tenant*, Ionesco is still drawing largely on his unconscious in these plays. This gives an added dimension, and of course a degree of ambiguity, for every element cannot be rationalized.

Bérenger's undertaking gives tremendous depth and power to this work, for the metaphysical proportions of his almost mythical adventure to conquer death make of him a quasi-religious hero, a kind of unconscious knight in quest of an enemy more enormous and more dangerous than he dreams. While his naïveté and unawareness refuse him the stature of tragic hero, his desire to destroy the Killer and restore happiness to mankind so that "springtime will return forever and all cities may be radiant," certainly makes of him a great humanitarian.

In *Rhinoceros* (1959) we meet Bérenger again, but it is a different Bérenger. Still naïve and innocent, he feels ill at ease with life and seeks comfort in drink. From the start he is contrasted sharply to his friend Jean, the dictatorial, self-important, frighteningly organized man of slogans and fixed ideas. Jean, it is clear, is a perfect target for ideologies that stifle individual thinking. Bérenger, on the other hand, is a nonbelonger. He recalls once again the man of the absurd, described by Camus in *The Myth of Sisyphus*, keenly aware of the meaninglessness of his dreary day-to-day existence. Instead of making a heroic revolt, however, Bérenger has chosen a kind of death in alcohol. It will not be until the play's end that he can choose—or perhaps be forced into—a more heroic commitment. Jean points out that he too must follow this regime, but he refuses to recognize the absurdity of his patterned life, and has buttressed himself with a form of religion, the religion of duty. He possesses the strength of the blind; that is to say, the strength of a rhinoceroslike animal with which discussion is impossible.

In these two characters Ionesco portrays what we may describe as the totalitarian mind on the one hand, and the un-committed on the other. Using them, and several dozen color-ful, amusing, caricaturelike personages, he treats the theme of ideas becoming ideologies and growing thence into epidemics until every trace of human feeling, individuality, or thinking is transformed into mass hysteria. The rhinoceros that appears in a French provincial town one Sunday morning seems strange, perhaps even a bit dangerous (it does after all flatten a cat), but it is not at first terrifying, and serves merely as matter for discussion, disquisition, and perplexity. It is only in the second act, when we discover that more and more people are becom-ing rhinoceroses, that we become alarmed and begin to pose more serious questions. In the amusing office scene Bérenger's colleagues take sides for and against the rhinoceroses and at-tempt to explain the strange phenomenon. But when Béren-ger's friend Jean is metamorphosed into a rhinoceros before our very eyes, and when Bérenger, attempting to escape his threatening horn, encounters rhinos on every side, the night-marish quality of his adventure becomes more apparent. Only one more act is necessary to show us the gradual demission of all his friends, including those who were most indignantly op-posed to the rhinocerization of others, leaving at last only Bérenger, the solitary human being surrounded by a sea of thick-skinned, trumpeting pachyderms. "I'm not capitulat-ing!" is his last pathetic cry.

The critical response to *Rhinoceros* was extremely varied. Ionesco's former detractors signed with relief, claiming that here at last was a comprehensible play in which he shows some political commitment. Others claimed that it was as incom-prehensible as ever. His earlier admirers disappointedly spoke of concessions, for some of them felt that *Rhinoceros* re-sembled the commercial theater. Indeed, it was the performance of this play that consecrated Ionesco by its performances at the Théâtre de France.

And yet, despite the apparent clarity with which Ionesco writes in *Rhinoceros*, is it indeed a committed political play? There is no denying that the major theme is one with political overtones, to say the least. Ionesco himself has said: "*Rhinoceros* is certainly an anti-Nazi play, yet it is also and mainly an attack on collective hysteria and the epidemics that lurk beneath the surface of reason and ideas." It would seem a mistake to make too specific an interpretation of the play. Like Ionesco's other works, this one derives a great deal of its meaning from the unconscious, and there are elements that cannot be logically "explained." One might even say that Bérenger is a remarkably weak personage to represent the human side in this conflict with the inhuman. Before his final cry of noncapitulation, indeed, he wonders why he cannot change and become like the others. But *Rhinoceros* is not a syllogism, and Bérenger is not a flat paper cutout serving only the purposes of a militant ideologist determined to show us that he alone is right. Indeed, one of Ionesco's most fervent supporters through the years, the distinguished writer Pierre-Aimé Touchard, feels that this play reveals a more general stand, and paradoxically, through its apparent political theme is really saying that Ionesco-Bérenger will not capitulate to his critics of a Leftist, Brechtian, or any other ideological persuasion who feel that he should write more committed plays and give us some positive program that we might, rhinolike, follow.

Whatever our reaction to the thematic content of *Rhinoceros*, it is undeniable that in this fable Ionesco reveals once again his brilliant originality of conception and his great gift for theatrical realization. Here is no dull political slogan play couched in flat, humorless language. Instead, Ionesco has imagined a shocking, vigorous, yet amusing central image, which in

[33]

addition to its purely theatrical values of presence and surprise possesses a real significance. Through this image—which is more than an image, for it is the very subject of the play—he arrives at that violence which he feels the theater of our day so notably lacks:

Artistic expression is too feeble, imagination is too impoverished to simulate the horror and the wonder of this life, or of death, too inadequate even to take stock of it.

In *Rhinoceros*, Ionesco has strengthened artistic expression and enriched imagination to a degree where they can reflect with real theatrical vigor the author's vision of life. Like the primitive theater he admires, Ionesco has found again the dramatic impact, the pure theatricality of the monstrous—a thing we have forgotten long since in the West. The grossly and grimly exaggerated can communicate more effectively than the primly imitative. The power and violence of what Ionesco has called the "unrounded corners" hits us at a level below the conscious intellect and appeals to our histrionic sensibility as words, and all that appeal to the waking intellect, cannot.

Ionesco has successfully created situations that on one level are clever and amusing, on another exercise an almost magical appeal to our deeply buried childlike love of theater, play, and transformation, and on yet another have a real significance in the context of his play. The metamorphosis of an entire people into rhinos—and particularly the scene in which Jean actually turns green, thick-skinned, begins to grunt, and grows a horn before the eyes of his astonished friend—is from the standpoints of theatrical effectiveness and of meaningful metaphor one of the most brilliantly conceived in drama of the mid-century.

While *Rhinoceros* has been praised and blamed for being more outspoken than earlier Ionesco plays, it contains definite ties with his earlier style. We can still recognize the dehumanized mechanical characters, the comic use of language to suggest its misuse and fossilization, and above all the proliferation of objects, which here, as in *The Chairs*, forms the central metaphor of the play.

The dramatic organization is a further illustration of the play's basic idea: a downhill plunge. The first act offers a large variety of characters (human), and a good deal of action in an outdoor setting. In the second we are inside, space has already become restricted, the characters are reduced and all belong to the same milieu, that of the office and the workaday world. As the rhinos continue to proliferate, the human element is of course eliminated, and in the third act there are only three characters, two of whom defect to the enemy before the play's end.

While Act Two ends in a terrifying crescendo of rhinocerization, Act Three is an act of solitude. It has been criticized for its length, and indeed it adds little to the action of the play. But it is necessary, of course, to show us how Bérenger will finally react to his situation. Perhaps the long scene with his colleague Dudard, which opens the act and does not exist at all in the story from which Ionesco drew the play, might have been compressed or reworked into a later scene.

Together, in a few moments, Bérenger and his girl friend Daisy live the twenty-five years of married life from honeymoon to misunderstanding. Left alone, Bérenger, after struggle, doubts, and hesitation, turns to the rhinos and utters his last heroic cry of defiance—a cry that is lacking in the story version and that gives a more dramatic ending to the play, a somewhat more positive ending, too, for unlike his pathetic brother in *The Killer*, this Bérenger does not give up. But is it necessary to think of Bérenger as a hero? He is simply a poor human being who, because he refuses to follow the crowd, makes the lonely discovery that he can never join the crowd, and then finds a certain strength in his individuality. After all, Ionesco has told us that in *The Killer* and *Rhinoceros* he is not passing judgment. He is simply telling a story of what happened to Bérenger, and he solicits interpretations, without necessarily accepting them all. Interpretations, not betrayals. In an article published in the French newspaper *Arts* in 1961, Ionesco expresses his surprise and disappointment in the American production of *Rhinoceros*, which he saw in its last stages of rehearsal. He denounces its lack of style, its intellectual dishonesty, and the effort to turn into riotous farce what the playwright considers to be above all a tragedy. From a "hard, fierce and disturbing" character, Jean had been changed into "a comic figure, a *feeble* rhinoceros." Boxing matches and other "cheap embellishment and decoration, unnecessary and therefore worthless," were introduced. And Ionesco adds a warning to his producers: "I am not writing literature. I am doing something quite different: I am writing drama. I mean that my text is not just dialogue, but also 'stage directions.' These should be respected as much as the text, they are essential, they are also sufficient."

Speaking to a group of the International Theater Institute in Helsinki in 1959 Ionesco declared, "I want no other limits than the technical limits of the stage machinery. People will say that my plays are music hall or circus. So much the better: let's bring in the circus!" *The Pedestrian of the Air* (1962) does just that, for it requires the use of rather complicated stage machinery to create the illusion of flying, and at one point in the play a circus arena appears onstage and Bérenger performs for the English audience. Here the Ionesco-Bérenger identification is almost unavoidable, for the hero of *The Pedestrian* is a playwright. Unfortunately, this gives him the opportunity, when interviewed by an English journalist, to express the author's ideas in terms that are much too explicit:

dislike of committed theater, mistrust of its advocates and of men who give in to history; need for inner renewal, for a theater whose terror and atrocity might match that of life; and fear of death, a fear that paralyzes him. But aside from this verbose opening section of the play (which of course has its interest, though in a strictly nontheatrical sense), *The Pedestrian of the Air* seems to mark a return to the earlier method of developing a simple situation as far as it will go, for, although lengthy, this one-act play relates an uncomplicated incident in the life of Bérenger: while in England with his wife and daughter, he goes out for a walk one day, and to the surprise of the English folk, such is his sense of happiness and well-being, he begins to walk in the air, and finally flies off, apparently into outer space, where he witnesses an apocalyptic vision of such terror and magnitude that he returns completely sobered. We note the familiar progression from euphoria to depression, dominated this time not by a proliferation on stage, but by the hideous revelation of endless nothingness, suffering and death in the abyss of life and time.

Despite certain obvious points the author hopes to make, it is clear that *The Pedestrian* is largely a projection of very personal dreams into free theatrical terms, a kind of fairy spectacle without fairies, as Henri Gouhier puts it. Against a background of the usual mechanical people, Ionesco creates another pathetic Chaplinesque character, not a superman, but surely a human being, who refuses to give in to the dehumanized elements of life. Just as Jack is the symbol of submission, the several Bérenger characters, M. Gouhier suggests, are symbolic of the refusal to submit to the pressures of society. Dominated by his dreams, happy in his natural state, Bérenger is not limited here by the physical. Man's nature, his memory, his dreams seem to point to a being perfectly integrated in nature, to whom flying, like walking, is second nature. He is at ease, he

[37]

is joyous in nature, before the wonders of creation. But, alas, Bérenger's story is simply one of wish fulfillment, for although he claims man can fly as high as infinity, his experience shows us that sooner or later he must bump his head against the sky and come tumbling down.

Bérenger's voyage into outer space is at the same time a voyage within, for he discovers a double reality: his own personal death as well as the possible annihilation of the human race. The paradise aflame, the Bosch-like visions of deformity and suffering, the bottomless pits and bombardments he sees—all suggest the terror of our atomic age, while the millions of stars exploding, the universes disappearing and the deserts of ice and fire are a frightening warning of things to come if we persevere in warlike ways.

The Pedestrian of the Air is, like all Ionesco's plays, rich in indirect commentary on a number of subjects. The couple comes in for some satire as the English couples, and above all Bérenger and his wife, show certain areas of incompatibility. As in earlier plays, the wife is more level-headed, unimaginative, embarrassed by the poetic and physical flights of her husband; and she attempts to hold him down to earth, dismissing his dreams as foolishness. His daughter however shares in his imaginings, which suggests of course that the poetic and the childlike are neighboring worlds.

It is also hinted that Bérenger's flight represents his inspiration, his writing. He flies because he is powerless to do otherwise, just as the dramatist writes perhaps without specific purpose, simply because it is his vocation to write. The Journalist, and John Bull, a particularly heavy and unimaginative character, feel there must be some other answer, some more serious reason for Bérenger's flight. Like the advocates of committed theater, they seek a purpose, for the gratuitous act of creation does not explain, or excuse, itself.

JOURNALIST. Why did you fly?
BÉRENGER. I don't know . . . I couldn't help it.
JOHN BULL. We mean, "why did you fly?" What were you trying to demonstrate by such a feat?
. . .

JOHN BULL. (*To the other Englishmen.*) At any rate, his feat isn't extraordinary at all. . . . Why take so much trouble when we can get to the other side of the valley in a few seconds simply by crossing the bridge in an automobile?

The practical man, who believes every action must serve an immediately useful purpose, will never understand the poetic flights of a Bérenger, the dreamer who vindicates the rights of the imagination, the validity of the artist and the visionary. He stands for a human universe, opposed to that frighteningly mechanized one represented by the gentleman who says, "Going back to natural ways of doing things is contrary to progress and to the evolution of the spirit."

The last words of *The Pedestrian* were originally those spoken by Bérenger: "Nothing more for the moment." However, before publishing the play Ionesco added a speech by Bérenger's daughter: "Perhaps the fires will go out, perhaps the ice will melt, perhaps the abysses will fill themselves up, perhaps . . . the gardens . . . the gardens . . ." Scarcely a hopeful ending, for at best it offers only a dim hope, and reminds us that the poets and the pure in heart, the simple and the innocent, have always dreamed of an earthly paradise. Here there is no affirmation, simply the wish that the garden might bloom again.

The explicit statements of Ionesco-Bérenger in the interview scene of *The Pedestrian* make it clear that Ionesco has reached a kind of impasse and is attempting to renew his inspiration. Paralyzed by the conviction that there is nothing to say, by the belief that literary activity must lead on to something else, and by a fear of death, he seems unable to find his direction. "I am paralyzed because I know I am going to die," says Bérenger. "I can no longer do anything. I want to be cured of death."

A few months later, in the fall of 1962, Ionesco turned to a play dealing above all with the theme of death, which has haunted him since his earliest years. While *The Pedestrian of the Air* treats of universal destruction and atomic annihilation, *The King Dies* (also known as *Exit the King*) describes more particularly a man's very personal reaction to his own death. But once again there is an element of ambiguity and it is strongly suggested that Bérenger I is more than a man, more than a king, perhaps mankind itself—that king dispossessed, as Pascal called him—and his agony a cosmic agony, as the universe settles back into dusty nothingness.

Bérenger I is to die, he is told, before the end of the spectacle, and the play is simply his long resistance to, and gradual acceptance of, that death. At first he cannot believe that he is to die *now*, but his doctor makes it very real with a small detail: "You will have no breakfast tomorrow morning." Suddenly, from an abstraction, death becomes something frighteningly concrete, for us as well as for Bérenger. The play is not so much a description as it is an experience of death. Rather than attempting to show us a detailed psychological portrait of a dying man, Ionesco draws us into the drama emotionally and forces us to experience the feeling of dying ourselves. He accomplishes this by creating a kind of archetypal dying king who is both human and mythical. Dealing with his profoundest obsession, Ionesco reaches a universal level, for death harasses all men: my own nonexistence is inconceivable.

The mythical figure is a kind of Prometheus and Fisher King in one. His decrepit guard outlines all the accomplishments of the dying King, who not only stole fire from the gods and invented steel, the airplane, the automobile, the plough, and the Eiffel Tower; he also wrote the *Iliad* and the *Odyssey* and is the mysterious figure masked by the name of Shakespeare. To accomplish all this Bérenger has, of course, lived for centuries, and his death would seem to mark the disappearance of the human race—or at any rate its temporary disappearance before another world arises, made possible by the sacrifice of the King. For like the Fisher King of the old Arthurian romances, and his antecedent in primitive fertility rites, Bérenger must die in order to release nature from death and sterility. In his kingdom not a blade of grass, not a lettuce leaf will grow as long as he is alive, but when he has accepted, his older wife says (he has a young wife as well), life will flourish again—but without him. Bérenger, then, keeps the faint heroic tinge given him in earlier plays, but he is a pathetic hero without the stature of his classical counterpart. He is no Oedipus seeking out the truth no matter what it means; he is a frightened man refusing to see the truth until it is absolutely forced upon him.

The mythical ambience is stressed in several scenes by a liturgical style employing chanting and gestures as the characters supplicate nature, the dead who have gone before, and the Great Nothingness, in order to help the King accept his death.

JULIETTE. You statues, you bright ones or dark ones, you ancient ones, you shadows, you memories.
MARIE. Teach him serenity.
GUARD. Teach him indifference.
DOCTOR. Teach him resignation.
MARGUERITE. Make him listen to reason, and calm him.
KING. You suicides, teach me what I must do to acquire disgust for life. Teach me lassitude.

Such a treatment certainly adds depth to the work, but it is by no means the only method Ionesco has used to enrich the meanings of his play. On another level, it strikes us as a kind of psychodrama whose action is all occurring within the very mind of the central character: the few personages of the play seem to represent different aspects of Bérenger himself, and when they no longer obey his commands, it is as though a certain part of himself had atrophied in the death agony. The young wife, Marie, represents wish-fulfillment, is the sweet voice of his id, perhaps, telling the King what he wants to hear, while the older wife, Marguerite, like some fateful mistress of ceremonies, constantly recalls the facts. The servant girl Juliette pops in and out like a subconscious image, and as the play draws to a close all the characters disappear one by one, as though aspirated into some cosmic vacuum cleaner, leaving the old King alone. For death is a lonely experience, and each man must die his own death in complete solitude. To Bérenger all his family now seem strangers, and when he tells them he is dying he cannot feel that he is saying what he wants to say, for he is merely "making literature."

Again the parellel with Ionesco himself is clear: the attempt to say something, when he feels that ultimately nothing can be said, results in paralysis and silence. "I have a mirror in my entrails," says Bérenger, recalling the dramatist's claim that his most personal obsessions are most universal. "Everything is reflected there," the King continues, "I can see more and more clearly, I see the world, I see life seeping away."

On the most apparent level, neither mythical nor subconscious, *The King Dies* relates the death of a man in basically realistic terms, if by realism we mean recognized, genuine emotion truthfully reflected. The progression from security to suspicion, from refusal to realization to slow acceptance, is told in moving terms. The two central characters, Bérenger and Marguerite, are rounded, reasonably complex people within the areas of their obsessions. They have a real existence, which is rare in Ionesco's theater. The surrounding characters, more schematic, are also more human than secondary characters in any of his other plays. Instead of the usual mechanical language with which the peripheral characters express themselves, they use more conventional stage language. Indeed, even the little servant expresses herself at times in a rather learned and eloquent manner, and it is Marie, who might have struck us as shallowly optimistic, who describes life as "a short walk through a flowery way, an unkept promise, a vanished smile."

The King Dies is indeed radically different from the early Ionesco, and even from the earlier Bérenger plays. Rather than one or two "human" characters surrounded by a group of caricatured subhumans, we find a nucleus of living characters with nothing on the periphery. The six characters of *The King Dies* are all onstage almost from beginning to end. Their language is not that familiar repetitious, nonrational, amusing speech. With few exceptions it is the speech of reasonably living human beings. Although at one point Ionesco indicates that they are to play in a tragic guignol style, for the most part their behavior is not pronouncedly fanciful. While the major theme of death and the minor one of the couple certainly recall early Ionesco, the treatment afforded them does not. With the exception of a few automatic cliché sentences and the "magical" disappearances of the characters and décor at the end of the play, this work is strangely different from previous ones. And yet it does not suggest a complete about-face, for the profound humanity of the author as he suffers for himself and for all men in the face of death is a constant, and despite robots and automatons could be glimpsed in warmly moving terms from as early as 1951 with *The Chairs*. Marguerite and Bérenger are a kind of latter-day Old Man and Old Woman, and the wife is still playing the role of mother as well as that of spouse. There is nothing more pathetically real, more moving, more nightmarish than the ending of *The King Dies*, as Marguerite, both nurse and Death herself, leads Bérenger to the face of his annihilation. Slowly she frees him of his attachment to life, despite his resistance, despite his sense of self. The magical, hallucinatory quality of this renunciation scene recalls the wooing scene between Jack and his three-nosed fiancée, but here the bride is Death. As even Marguerite is sucked into nothingness, and Bérenger remains alone on his throne, the walls of the room fall away, leaving the solitary King bathed in a gray light. Then the King and his throne are slowly swallowed in shadow and mist, and only the gray, empty stage remains.

"Useless agitation, wasn't it?" asks Marguerite before she disappears. Is this a comment by Ionesco on his own dramaturgic activity? In the two years since completing *The King Dies*, he has written no new plays. His prolonged silence, which is after all nothing new, may be the prelude to a renewal. Or it may mean that, overcome by his own obsessions and fears, by the time-consuming activities of a world-famous author, and by the adverse comments of critics, he has indeed reached an impasse. If such is the case, it will be a real loss for the contemporary theatrical world, for Ionesco has been one of the moving spirits in the renewal of theater in the middle of the twentieth century, and his dramatic output in fourteen years of activity, from 1949 to 1962, reveals him as one of the most original dramatists alive today. His exceptionally lucid essays, manifesting a profound understanding of the problems of theater, lead one to hope that he will continue both as dramatist and as essayist to point the way to a new concept of theater which, in content and in form, stands for freedom of the dramatist as it does for freedom of mankind.

SELECTED BIBLIOGRAPHY

PRINCIPAL WORKS OF EUGÈNE IONESCO

Théâtre, I. Paris, Gallimard, 1954. (Includes La Cantatrice chauve, La Leçon, Jacques ou la Soumission, Les Chaises, Victimes du devoir, Amédée ou Comment s'en débarrasser.)
Théâtre, II. Paris, Gallimard, 1958. (Includes L'Impromptu de l'Alma, Tueur sans gages, Le Nouveau Locataire, L'Avenir est dans les oeufs, Le Maître, Jeune fille à marier.)
Rhinocéros. Paris, Gallimard, 1959.
La Photo du Colonel, récits. Paris, Gallimard, 1962. (Includes "Oriflamme," "La Photo du Colonel," "Le Piéton de l'air," "Une Victime du devoir," "Rhinocéros," "LaVase," "Printemps 1939.")
Notes et contre-notes. Paris, Gallimard, 1962.
Théâtre, III. Paris, Gallimard, 1963. (Includes Rhinocéros, Le Piéton de l'air, Délire à deux, Le Tableau, Scène à quatre, Les Salutations, La Colère.)
Le Roi se meurt. Paris, Gallimard, 1963.

Translations of Ionesco's Works

Four Plays. Tr. Donald M. Allen. New York, Grove, 1958. (Includes The Bald Soprano; The Lesson; Jack, or The Submission; The Chairs.)
Amédée, The New Tenant, Victims of Duty. Tr. Donald Watson. New York, Grove, 1958.
The Killer and Other Plays. Tr. Donald Watson. New York, Grove, 1960. (Includes The Killer; Improvisation, or The Shepherd's Chameleon; Maid to Marry.)
Rhinoceros and Other Plays. Tr. Derek Prouse. New York, Grove, 1960. (Includes Rhinoceros, The Leader, The Future is in Eggs.)
Notes and Counter Notes. Tr. Donald Watson. New York, Grove, 1964.
Plays, V. Tr. Donald Watson. London, Calder, 1963. (Includes Exit the King, Foursome, The Motor Show.)
The Motor Show. Tr. Donald Watson. *Evergreen Review*, No. 32 (April–May, 1964).

Barbour, Thomas. "Beckett and Ionesco," *Hudson Review*, 11 (Summer, 1958), 271–77.

Cahiers des Saisons (Ionesco issue), 15 (Winter, 1959).

Cahiers Renaud-Barrault (Rhinocéros issue), 29 (February, 1960); (Piéton de l'air issue), 42 (February, 1963).

Coe, Richard N. Ionesco. New York, Grove, 1961.

Daniel, John T. "Ionesco and the Ritual of Nihilism," *Drama Survey*, 1:1 (1961), 54–65.

Doubrovsky, J. S. "Ionesco and the Comedy of Absurdity," *Yale French Studies*, 23 (Summer, 1959), 3–10.

Dukore, Bernard. "The Theatre of Ionesco: A Union of Form and Substance," *Educational Theatre Journal*, 13 (1961), 174–81.

Eastman, Richard M. "Experiment and Vision in Ionesco's Plays," *Modern Drama*, 4 (1961), 3–19.

Esslin, Martin. The Theatre of the Absurd. Garden City, N.Y., Doubleday, 1961.

Fowlie, Wallace. Dionysus in Paris. New York, Meridian, 1960.

——— "New Plays of Ionesco and Genet," *Tulane Drama Review*, V, 1 (1960), 43–48.

Glicksberg, Charles I. "Ionesco and the Aesthetics of the Absurd," *Arizona Quarterly*, 18 (1962), 293–303.

Grossvogel, David I. Four Playwrights and a Postscript. Ithaca, N.Y., Cornell University Press, 1962.

Guicharnaud, Jacques. Modern French Theatre from Giraudoux to Beckett. New Haven, Conn., Yale University Press, 1961.

——— "The 'R' Effect," *L'Esprit Créateur*, 2:4 (Winter, 1962), 159–65.

Knowles, Dorothy. "Ionesco and the Mechanisms of Language," *Modern Drama*, 6 (1962), 7–10.

Lamont, Rosette C. "The Metaphysical Farce: Beckett and Ionesco," *French Review*, 31 (February, 1959), 319–28.

——— "The Proliferation of Matter in Ionesco's Plays," *L'Esprit Créateur*, 2:4 (1962), 189–97.

Pronko, Leonard C. "The Anti-Spiritual Victory in the Theater of Ionesco," *Modern Drama*, 2:1 (May, 1959), 29–35.

——— Avant-Garde: The Experimental Theater in France. Berkeley, Calif., University of California Press, 1962.

——— "Modes and Means of the Avant-Garde Theatre," *Bucknell Review*, 12:2 (May, 1964), 46–56.

———— "The Prelate and the Pachyderm: Rear Guard and Vanguard Drama in the French Theatre," *Modern Drama*, 4:1 (May, 1961), 63–71.

Reed, Muriel. "Ionesco," *Réalités*, 85 (December, 1957), 44–50.

Tulane Drama Review (Ionesco and Genet issue), VII, 3 (Spring, 1963).

Valency, Maurice. "Flight into Lunacy," *Theatre Arts*, 44:8 (August, 1960), 8–9, 68–69.

Watson, Donald. "The Plays of Ionesco," *Tulane Drama Review*, IV, 1 (1958), 48–53.

Wellwarth, George E. The Theater of Protest and Paradox: Developments in the Avant-Garde Drama. New York, New York University Press, 1964.

Yale French Studies (New dramatists issue), 29 (1962).

COLUMBIA ESSAYS ON MODERN WRITERS

EDITOR: William York Tindall

ADVISORY EDITORS:

Jacques Barzun, W.T.H. Jackson, Joseph A. Mazzeo, Justin O'Brien

84
I64

Each pamphlet, 65 cents. Orders accepted only for 6 or more pamphlets, same or assorted titles.

Distributed in the United Kingdom and in Europe by
Columbia University Press, Ltd., 6a Bedford Square, London W.C.1
U.K. price: 5s net

Order from your bookseller or from

COLUMBIA UNIVERSITY PRESS

2960 Broadway, New York, NY 10027